DISCOVER DENVER

A Travel Guide To The Mile High City

Franca Benevente

Copyright © 2024 Franca Benevente

All rights reserved

The characters and events portrayed in this book are fictitious. Any similarity to real persons, living or dead, is coincidental and not intended by the author.

No part of this book may be reproduced, or stored in a retrieval system, or transmitted in any form or by any means, electronic, mechanical, photocopying, recording, or otherwise, without express written permission of the publisher.

ISBN: 9798329859331

Cover design by: Art Painter
Library of Congress Control Number: 2018675309
Printed in the United States of America

Wherever you go, go with your heart

CONFUCIUS

CONTENTS

Title Page
Copyright
Epigraph
Introduction — 1
Chapter 1: Getting to Denver — 3
Chapter 2: Where to Stay — 10
Chapter 3: Top Attractions — 18
Chapter 4: Get Outdoors — 26
Chapter 5: Cultural and Historical Sites — 30
Chapter 6: Family-Friendly Activities — 34
Chapter 7: Food and Drink Scene — 38
Chapter 8: Shopping in Denver — 47
Chapter 9: Arts and Entertainment — 51
Chapter 10: Day Trips and Excursions — 58
Chapter 11: Safety Tips and Local Etiquette — 61
Conclusion — 64
Resources — 66

INTRODUCTION

Welcome to Denver, the Mile-High City, where urban life meets outdoor adventure. Nestled at an elevation of 5,280 feet at the base of the majestic Rocky Mountains, Denver offers a blend of cultural experiences, stunning natural beauty, and vibrant city neighborhoods. Whether you are a first-time visitor or a seasoned traveler, this simple guide will help you uncover the best of what Denver has to offer in one space. From top attractions and hidden gems to the best places to eat and stay, with a blend of local knowledge and a bit of research, I've compiled a great list for all travelers to enjoy.

My name is Franca Benevente, and 15 years ago I moved from the warm, sun kissed beaches of Florida to the majestic mountain peaks of Colorado. My husband and I, along with our one year old baby took a leap of faith into the (very cold) unknown. It started as a five year plan, and here we are, 15 years later. It's been an amazing and transformative journey for both of us and our now 2 children, one born and raised right here in Denver–a true Colorado native–I hear those are hard to come by these days! Besides the amazing natural beauty of Colorado and the wonderful community of friends we've established, we have fallen in love with Denver's lively culture and eclectic art and music scene. (Red Rocks is one of my favorite places on earth!) Let's set off exploring the diverse and dynamic cityscape of Denver. Whatever adventure you choose...I've got you covered!*

*The information provided in this travel guide is intended for general informational purposes only. While every effort has been made to ensure the accuracy and completeness of the content, the author and publisher make no guarantees regarding the currentness, reliability, or suitability of the information contained herein. Travel conditions, accomodations, local businesses, and attractions can change frequently, and readers are encouraged to verify details independently before making travel plans. Travelers should also consider any potential travel advisories and health and safety guidelines relevant to their destination.

View of Downtown Denver

CHAPTER 1: GETTING TO DENVER

Best Time To Visit

Denver is a year-round destination, but the best time to visit depends on your interests. Each season will offer a unique experience. The weather is relatively mild year-round, but always be sure to pack layers since it can change pretty quickly. A hot summer day can quickly turn into a cold, windy evening. A few essentials such as a jacket or sweater, a warm hat, and closed shoes can come in handy, even in the warmer months.

Spring (March to May)

This is a lovely time with (mostly) mild weather and cooler nights, there's lots of blooming flowers, large shady trees, and also fewer crowds. There may be an occasional snowstorm in April (or even May!) but for the most part, it's a perfect time for sight-seeing, exploring the city's parks and gardens, as well as taking advantage of outdoor activities.

Summer (June to August)

Summer offers warm, often very sunny days and cooler nights with the occasional rain (or hail) storm. It's ideal for hiking, mountain biking, attending outdoor festivals and concerts or enjoying dining al fresco at one of Denver's outdoor dining patios. It's a popular time for tourists, so you can expect more crowded attractions.

Fall (September to November)

Fall in Denver is stunning and my personal favorite time of year, with vibrant fall foliage and pleasant temperatures. It's also a great time for hiking or taking a scenic drive into the mountains and enjoying the changing colors of the leaves and the crisp mountain air.

Scenic Fall Foliage in Colorado

Winter (December to February)

Winter brings snow and much colder temperatures, making it a prime season for skiing and snowboarding at one of the many surrounding picturesque ski resorts. Regardless, most winter days are still sunny and the snow tends to melt pretty quickly. Denver itself is festive during the holiday season, with plenty of winter activities like immersive light shows, gourmet dining, shopping, ice-skating, and visiting museums.

Denver City and County Building holiday lights

Transportation Options

Denver is easily accessible by air, rail, and road.

By Air

Denver International Airport: DIA is one of the busiest airports in the United States, serving as a major hub with flights from all around the world. It is located about 25 miles northeast of downtown Denver. Several major airlines operate here, providing both domestic and international flights. If you have time, DIA also offers plenty of options for local and national dining, shopping, and self-care services, as well as rotating public art exhibits. As you exit or enter DIA by car, don't forget to look out for our towering 32 foot blue fiberglass horse with glowing red eyes guarding the airport, lovingly known as "Blucifer" by the locals.

The Mustang "Blucifer" at DIA

By Train

The Amtrak station is located at the historic Union Station in the heart of downtown Denver, providing convenient access to the city's public transportation network.

By Road

Many visitors choose to drive to Denver, taking advantage of the extensive interstate highway system. This option provides flexibility and the opportunity to explore surrounding areas and scenic routes, great for a road trip!

Interstate Highways:

I-25: Runs north-south through Denver, connecting the city to Colorado Springs to the south and Fort Collins to the north.

I-70: Runs east-west through Denver, connecting the city to the mountains and ski resorts to the west and to Kansas to the east.

I-76: Connects Denver to northeastern Colorado and continues into Nebraska.

By Bus Services

Greyhound offers long-distance bus services connecting Denver to various cities across the country.

Megabus: Provides affordable bus services to and from Denver, covering several major cities.

By Shuttle Services

Various shuttle services operate between Denver International Airport and downtown Denver, as well as other locations in the metro area. These include shared-ride shuttles, private car services, and hotel shuttles. Several companies offer mountain shuttle services from Denver to nearby mountain resorts and attractions, making it easy for visitors to reach the ski resorts without needing to rent a car.

Navigating The City

Once in Denver, there are plenty of options for getting around. Downtown Denver and many surrounding neighborhoods are definitely walkable/bikeable, but the area is expansive and it would benefit travelers to use other modes of transportation if they want to explore beyond the city limits.

Regional Transportation District (RTD)

RTD is the primary local transportation system. RTD offers an extensive network of light rail and bus services that connect Denver to nearby cities and suburbs. Travelers can also take the airport rail (known as the A-Line) to and from

DIA and Union Station.

Car Rentals

Conveniently rent a car directly from one of several car rental companies located on site at the Denver International Airport or throughout the metro Denver area. Although, if you do choose to drive, be prepared since traffic downtown can get pretty crowded and parking is expensive.

Rideshare

Rideshare options like Uber and Lyft are widely available and operate extensively in Denver, offering convenient and flexible transportation options for getting around the city and surrounding areas.

Bike or Electric Scooter

For a unique experience, consider renting an e-scooter or a bike to explore the city's bike-friendly streets. Denver has welcomed many bike and electric scooter companies and it's become a favorite way to explore the city for both locals and visitors.

CHAPTER 2: WHERE TO STAY

Denver is home to several lively and diverse neighborhoods, each offering unique attractions and experiences. Here are some of the coolest neighborhoods to visit and why:

LoDo (Lower Downtown)

LoDo is Denver's oldest neighborhood and the city's historic heart. It's known for its beautiful, restored Victorian buildings, lively nightlife, and an abundance of restaurants, bars, and shops. I love visiting Union Station for a bite to eat or a cold craft beer while sitting in the eclectic lounge area to people-watch. LoDo is home to some of Denver's major attractions, making it a perfect area for both day and night activities.

LoDo highlights: Union Station, Coors Field, Museum of Contemporary Art Denver, Larimer Square, Market Street, Wynkoop Brewing Company, 16th Street Mall

RiNo (River North Art District)

RiNo is a haven for art lovers, featuring a mix of art galleries, studios, and colorful street murals, which makes it one of my favorite places to walk around. It's also known for its craft breweries, hip eateries, and live music venues.

RiNo highlights: Street art and murals, The Source, Denver Central Market, craft breweries

Mural in RiNo Neighborhood

Highlands

The Highlands neighborhood has a trendy mix of historic homes, chic boutiques, and cozy coffee shops. It offers stunning views of the downtown skyline and is a great place to explore local cuisine with its numerous restaurants and bars.

Highlands highlights: Highland Bridge, Little Man Ice Cream, Avanti Food & Beverage, Highlands Square

Cherry Creek

Cherry Creek is an upscale neighborhood known for its high-end shopping and dining options. The area features Cherry Creek Shopping Center and Cherry Creek North, an open-air shopping district with boutiques, galleries, and fine dining. Cherry Creek also has many beautiful parks and bike trails.

Cherry Creek highlights: Cherry Creek Shopping Center, Cherry Creek Trail, seasonal Cherry Creek Arts Festival

Cap Hill (Capitol Hill)

Capitol Hill is a boho neighborhood with a rich history and eclectic vibe. It's home to historic mansions, museums, and diverse dining options. The neighborhood also has a vibrant LGBTQ+ community.

Capitol Hill highlights: Colorado State Capitol, Molly Brown House Museum, Cheesman Park, Colfax Avenue

Capitol Hill Neighborhood Street

Five Points

Five Points has a deep cultural and musical heritage. It's historically significant for its African American culture and jazz music. The area has undergone revitalization and now features trendy eateries and breweries.

Five Points highlights: Black American West Museum, Five Points Jazz Festival, historic jazz venues

SoBo (South Broadway)

South Broadway is known for its hip and diverse atmosphere. It's a great place to explore vintage shops, music venues, and quirky bars. The area has a lively nightlife and I really enjoy the creative community vibe.

South Broadway highlights: Antique Row, The Hi-Dive music venue, Mayan Theatre, unique boutiques, popular night clubs.

Golden Triangle Creative District

This district is the cultural hub of Denver, home to numerous museums, galleries, and cultural institutions. It's a must-visit for art and history enthusiasts.

Golden Triangle Creative District highlights: Denver Art Museum, History Colorado Center, Clyfford Still Museum, Kirkland Museum of Fine & Decorative Art

Each of these neighborhoods offers a distinct slice of Denver's rich and varied culture, making them all worthy of a visit during your stay in the Mile High City.

Hotels, Vacation Rentals, Or Hostels

Denver visitors will have a large number of terrific accommodation options with a variety of prices. The price of a hotel can vary by amenities, dates, and neighborhood. These are just a few recommendations based on your budget.

Luxury Hotels

The Ritz-Carlton, Four Seasons Hotel Denver, The Brown Palace Hotel and Spa, The Ramble Hotel

The Brown Palace Hotel and Spa

Mid-Range Hotels

Kimpton Hotel Born, Hyatt Regency Denver, The Maven Hotel, Mint House, The Rally Hotel

Budget Options

Hostel Fish, Ember Hostel, Avenue Hostel, and various Airbnb options.

Unique Accommodations

The Crawford Hotel (inside Union Station), The ART, The Maven, The Curtis, historic inns like The Patterson Inn. During the warmer months, hotels with a rooftop terrace are always a great choice as well.

Vacation Rentals

Staying at an Airbnb or VRBO (Vacation Rental By Owner) can offer several advantages compared to traditional hotels. Vacation rentals can provide a more personalized experience. You can choose from a wide range of properties, including apartments, houses, and even my personal favorite, a home surrounded by nature and wildlife in one of the nearby mountain towns. This is a great option for larger families or groups and can be more cost-effective.

Bonus: Bring Your Dog

Denver is a very dog-friendly city, and there are dozens of pet-friendly activities and destinations, including dog-friendly hotels and dog parks. These include The Crawford, The Curtis, Hotel Teatro, The Maven Hotel, and many more!

Denver truly offers a wide range of accommodation choices for your stay depending on your budget and personal preferences. Whether you are looking for luxurious, boutique style, modern, trendy, quirky, lots of space, or privacy you'll be sure to find a lot of options.

CHAPTER 3: TOP ATTRACTIONS

Denver has many top attractions that cater to diverse interests. Visitors and locals alike find endless opportunities for venturing out and discovering what it has to offer.

Union Station

A historic landmark and transportation hub, Union Station is also a bustling and eclectic gathering place with restaurants, shops, and a boutique hotel. It's the perfect starting point for your Denver adventures and usually the first stop I make with my guests when heading downtown.

Denver's Union Station

Denver Art Museum

A must-visit for art lovers, the Denver Art Museum has an impressive collection of Native American art, contemporary pieces, and rotating exhibitions. The striking architecture alone is worth the visit.

Denver Art Museum

Denver Botanic Gardens

An oasis in the city, the Denver Botanic Gardens features 23 acres of diverse gardens, including a Japanese Garden, a tropical conservatory, and a rooftop garden. It's a perfect spot to take a stroll or have a picnic.

Denver Botanic Gardens

Denver Museum of Nature & Science

This museum offers interactive exhibits on everything from space exploration to dinosaur fossils. It's educational and entertaining for visitors of all ages. My family has been enjoying visiting this museum for years.

Denver Zoo

Home to over 3,500 animals, the Denver Zoo is a great family-friendly attraction. I took my children here often for many years while they were growing up. It's fun for grown-ups too and provides a little escape from the big city.

Colorado State Capitol

Take a free tour of the Colorado State Capitol, where you can stand exactly one mile above sea level and enjoy panoramic views from the beautiful golden dome.

Colorado State Capitol

Coors Field

Baseball fans should catch a Colorado Rockies game at Coors Field. The stadium offers stunning views of the Rocky Mountains, a roof-top bar, and an overall fun atmosphere. We enjoy several games during baseball season since ticket prices tend to be more affordable and more available than other sports venues.

Coors Field

Empower Field at Mile High

Home of our Denver Broncos, this stadium is a must-visit for football fans. Attend an exciting football game with our die-hard fans, or you plan to take a tour, giving you a behind-the-scenes look at the facilities. Denverites take their sports seriously, so it's best to purchase tickets ahead of time for football, basketball, and hockey games.

Red Rocks Park and Amphitheatre

No visit to Denver would be complete without going to Red Rocks Park and Amphitheatre. Located in Morrison, Colorado, just 15 miles west of Denver. Visitors can sight-see, hike, or dine during the day or attend a concert in the evening. This stunning natural amphitheater is carved out of massive red sandstone formations, creating a breathtaking backdrop and exceptional acoustics that make it one of the most iconic and sought-after performance spaces in the world. I have been fortunate enough to attend several concerts here. Truly one of my favorite places in the Denver area.

Red Rocks Amphitheatre, Morrison Colorado

Bonus: More Denver Staples to Visit

McGregor Square

Home of The Rally Hotel, the official hotel of the Colorado rockies, check out this dynamic one-block area to dine, shop, or attend one the many festivals and outdoor events.

The Denver Mint

Take a free tour of The Denver Mint. It's one of a handful of facilities that produces US currency, and one of only two (along with the US Mint in Philadelphia) that offers tours to the public.

The Cathedral Basilica of the Immaculate Conception

Attend a mass or simply stop in to this stunning Roman Catholic church located in the Capital Hill community.

The Cathedral Basilica of the Immaculate Conception

CHAPTER 4: GET OUTDOORS

City Park

One of Denver's largest parks, City Park offers the zoo, museum, a golf course, and paddle boating on Ferril Lake. It's a great spot for a day of family fun. In the summer months, hang with locals and enjoy City Park Jazz, a free summer concert series, where we gather to enjoy live jazz music in a relaxed atmosphere.

City Park Denver

Washington Park

Locals love "Wash Park" for its expansive lawns, flower gardens, and scenic lakes. Rent a bike or a paddle boat to explore or simply just relax in nature

Cheesman Park

This historic park is perfect for a relaxing day outdoors. It's surrounded by beautiful homes and offers great spots for picnicking and people-watching.

Confluence Park

A great spot for kayaking, tubing, or just relaxing by the river. It's also a popular spot for locals to enjoy the outdoors.

Red Rocks Park

Red Rocks is not just a concert venue, and has many scenic trails that visitors are free to walk or hike during the day. Sight-see and take lots of beautiful pictures while you're here exploring.

The Mother Cabrini Shrine

Located at the foothills of Golden, Colorado this shrine is a spiritual retreat and pilgrimage site dedicated to Saint Frances Xavier Cabrini. It features a variety of attractions, most notably the Statue of the Sacred Heart of Jesus, a 22-foot statue that stands atop a 373-step staircase. The climb is truly worth it and the views from the top are spectacular. It's not only a place of religious significance, but truly a tranquil retreat and always offers me a sense of peace and reflection when I visit.

Cherry Creek Reservoir

One of many reservoirs in the Denver area, located in Cherry Creek State Park, this reservoir is popular for boating, fishing, swimming, and even camping. The surrounding park offers extensive trails for hiking and biking.

Mount Evans Scenic Byway

Take a drive up the highest paved road in North America to the summit of Mount Evans. Enjoy breathtaking views, alpine lakes, and the chance to see mountain goats and bighorn sheep.

Mount Evans Scenic Byway

Day Trips to Rocky Mountain National Park

Just a short drive from Denver, Rocky Mountain National Park offers hiking, wildlife watching, and stunning mountain vistas. Trail Ridge Road is a highlight, taking you through some of the park's most beautiful landscapes.

Rocky Mountain National Park

CHAPTER 5: CULTURAL AND HISTORICAL SITES

Denver's history is definitely woven into its neighborhoods, landmarks, and cultural institutions. Visitors have plenty of opportunities to get immersed in Denver's rich history.

Larimer Square

Denver's oldest and most historic block, Larimer Square is now a bustling area filled with shops, restaurants, and nightlife. Its Victorian buildings and string lights make it a picturesque spot to explore. I love taking visitors for a stroll and a bite to eat to this iconic area of Denver.

Larimer Square

Molly Brown House Museum

Step back in time at the home of Titanic survivor Molly Brown. The museum offers guided tours that delve into her fascinating life and the history of Denver.

The Molly Brown House Museum

Black American West Museum

Learn about the history of African American pioneers in the West. The museum is housed in the former home of Dr. Justina Ford, Denver's first African American female doctor.

History Colorado Center

Interactive exhibits bring Colorado's history to life at this state-of-the-art museum. It's a great place to learn about the state's diverse cultural heritage.

Clyfford Still Museum

Art enthusiasts will appreciate this museum dedicated to the works of abstract expressionist painter Clyfford Still. The museum's architecture and layout provide an immersive experience.

CHAPTER 6: FAMILY-FRIENDLY ACTIVITIES

C hildren's Museum of Denver

With hands-on exhibits and interactive play areas, the Children's Museum is perfect for kids. I spent most of my early years in Denver bringing my kids here. Kids can climb, build, create, and explore in a fun and educational environment.

Denver Aquarium

Discover underwater worlds at the Denver Aquarium, featuring a variety of marine life, a mermaid show, and a rainforest exhibit. It's a great spot for a family day.

Denver Aquarium

Elitch Gardens Theme and Water Park

Attending "Elitches" is one of my kids favorite summertime activities. Visitors can enjoy thrilling rides, water slides, and family-friendly attractions. It's the perfect theme park for a day of fun and excitement.

Elitch Gardens and Empower Field in the background

Butterfly Pavilion

Get up close with butterflies, spiders, and other insects at the Butterfly Pavilion. It's a unique and educational experience for kids and adults alike.

Adventure Golf and Raceway

Challenge your family to a game of mini-golf, go-kart racing, or bumper cars at this fun-filled amusement center.

Meow Wolf Denver

Meow Wolf Denver is an immersive experience that offers a multi-sensory journey through a series of fantastical and surreal environments, each exhibit is designed by a diverse group of artists. Visitors can explore rooms, corridors, and spaces filled with vibrant colors, sounds, and interactive elements.

Meow Wolf Denver

CHAPTER 7: FOOD AND DRINK SCENE

Denver has a thriving food scene with so many excellent restaurants, known for its unique culinary offerings and the top notch craft beer. Here are some iconic foods, restaurants and breweries you can enjoy while in Denver.

Iconic Denver Foods

- **Green Chile:** A local favorite, green chile is a must-try. Made with roasted green chiles, pork, and various spices, enjoy it as a stew or smothered over burritos, fries or burgers. Green Chile is a beloved dish in Denver's Mexican and Southwestern cuisine.
- **Denver Omelet:** Served by many diners and restaurants, this classic omelet is a staple breakfast meal made with eggs, diced ham, onions, and green bell peppers
- **Bison Burgers:** Reflecting Colorado's ranching heritage, bison burgers are a leaner alternative to beef, and can be found in many local restaurants. My husband actually prefers bison burgers over

traditional beef burgers.

- **Smothered Burritos:** These are often very large and filled with meats, beans and cheese, then usually covered in green chile sauce. They are a staple in Denver's Mexican and Tex-mex restaurants and one of my favorite iconic foods.

Smothered Burrito covered in green chile

- **Paletas:** These traditional Mexican ice pops come in lots of flavors from fruity to creamy and are a refreshing treat available in many local shops.
- **Rocky Mountain Oysters:** For the adventurous eater, these deep-fried bull calf testicles are a Colorado specialty. Honestly, I personally have never had the courage to try this famous regional delicacy!

Best Breakfast Spots

- **Snooze, an A.M. Eatery:** Famous for their creative twist and breakfast and brunch cocktails. There will be a line, so plan ahead.
- **Lucile's Creole Cafe:** Enjoy a charming southern-style breakfast with beignets, shrimp and grits and chicory coffee.
- **Jelly Cafe:** A quirky cafe known for their homemade donuts and inventive breakfast dishes. And retro decor.
- **The Universal:** Known for its comfort food and friendly atmosphere, The universal serves up delicious dishes like cornbread rancheros and their famous griddle cakes.

Bonus: Any local diner

Among local favorites are classics like Swift's Breakfast House, Chef Zorba's and the Butcher Block Cafe with its famed cinnamon rolls. If you're craving early-morning comfort food, a solid Denver diner can't be beat.

Lunch And Dinner Recommendations

- **Root Down:** A farm-to-table restaurant offering globally inspired dishes with a focus on sustainability and local ingredients.

Outside of Root Down Restaurant-Denver

- **Mercantile Dining & Provision**: Located in Union Station, it offers a market and a dining experience in one. This spot offers a farm-to-table menu featuring dishes like house-made pastas, fresh seafood, and unique small plates.
- **Hop Alley:** Modern Chinese cuisine with a twist in the RiNo Art District.
- **Tavernetta:** A beautiful Italian restaurant known for its exquisite pasta dishes, fresh seafood, and warm, inviting atmosphere. The wine selection is also top-notch.
- **The Wolf's Tailor:** An intimate, stylish spot blending Italian and Japanese influences. The tasting menu changes regularly, featuring seasonal and locally-sourced ingredients.
- **El Five:** Offering stunning views of the city skyline, El Five serves up a Mediterranean tapas menu with dishes inspired by Spain, the Middle East, and North Africa. Their paella and lamb ribs are highly recommended.

- **Safta:** Located in The Source Hotel, Safta specializes in modern Israeli cuisine. The hummus, pita, and lamb ragu are must-tries, and the brunch menu is also fantastic.
- **Beckon:** An intimate, reservation-only restaurant offering a seasonal tasting menu. Each dish is meticulously crafted and beautifully presented, making for a memorable fine dining experience.
- **Bar Dough:** An Italian-inspired restaurant with a focus on wood-fired pizzas, house-made pastas, and small plates. The gnocchi and Brussels sprouts are particularly popular.
- **Rioja:** Located in Larimer Square, Rioja serves Mediterranean-inspired cuisine with a focus on fresh, local ingredients. The artichoke tortelloni and lamb loin are standout dishes.
- **Guard and Grace:** A modern steakhouse known for its high-quality meats and stylish setting. In addition to steaks, the menu features a variety of seafood and vegetarian options.
- **Annette:** A cozy spot in Aurora's Stanley Marketplace, Annette offers a menu of elevated comfort food with a focus on wood-fired cooking. The roasted chicken and deviled eggs are local favorites.
- **Mizuna:** An elegant French-American restaurant offering a seasonal menu with dishes like lobster mac and cheese and beef Wellington. The intimate setting and excellent service make it perfect for special occasions.
- **Carmine's on McGregor Square:** Carmine's is a contemporary-chic lunch and dinner restaurant specializing in family-style plates of Italian-American food. Make sure to save room for a taste of the homemade

limoncello.

Food Markets And Street Food

- **Denver Central Market:** A gourmet marketplace with various vendors offering everything from fresh seafood to artisan chocolates.
- **The Source:** A food hall in a former foundry building, featuring local vendors and a brewery.
- **Civic Center EATS:** A seasonal event featuring food trucks and live music in Civic Center Park.
- **The Stanley Marketplace:** mixed-use urban marketplace with a variety of retail options, including boutiques, gift shops, restaurants, and a zero-waste market. It includes over 50 independently owned Colorado businesses under one roof, as well as a public park.

Bonus: Local Favorites

Denverites have a wide variety of palettes and there's no shortage of diverse local favorites to eat. Here's a few: Angelo's Taverna, Sushi Den, Katsu Ramen, Chef Zorbas, Chubby's, Hop Alley, any Vietnamese and Thai Cuisine on Federal Blvd

Denver's Craft Beer Scene

- **Great Divide Brewing Company:** One of Denver's most well-known breweries, Great Divide offers a wide range of beers, from their famous Yeti Imperial Stout to refreshing seasonal brews. The taproom in RiNo (River North Art District) is a great place to sample their offerings.

- **Denver Beer Co.:** Known for its laid-back atmosphere and creative beers, Denver Beer Co. is a favorite among locals. Their Graham Cracker Porter and Incredible Pedal IPA are popular choices. The brewery has a large outdoor patio perfect for enjoying a sunny day.
- **Wynkoop Brewing Company:** Colorado's first brewpub, Wynkoop is housed in a historic building in LoDo (Lower Downtown). They offer a variety of beers, including unique options like the Rocky Mountain Oyster Stout.
- **Ratio Beerworks:** Also located in RiNo, Ratio Beerworks combines a love for music and beer. Their rooftop patio is a great spot to enjoy their diverse range of beers, from IPAs to lagers.
- **Trve Brewing Co.:** A metal-themed brewery on Broadway, Trve is known for its innovative sour and wild ales. The dark and moody atmosphere is a unique setting to try their creative brews.
- **Crooked Stave Artisan Beer Project:** Specializing in wild and sour ales, Crooked Stave offers a distinctive beer experience. Their Barrel Cellar in The Source is a great place to taste their complex, barrel-aged beers.
- **Black Shirt Brewing Co.:** This brewery in RiNo focuses on red ales, offering a variety of styles within that category. Their outdoor beer garden often features live music and food trucks.
- **Blue Moon Brewing Company:** While Blue Moon is now a national brand, its roots are in Denver. The brewery in RiNo offers experimental and limited-

release beers alongside their classic Belgian White.

Blue Moon Brewing Company

Bonus: Beer Festivals

- **The Great American Beer Festival:** Held annually in Denver, is the premier beer event in the U.S., featuring thousands of beers from hundreds of breweries.
- **Collaboration Fest:** Showcasing unique collaborations between breweries, this festival is a celebration of the cooperative spirit of the craft beer community.
- **Denver Beer Fest:** A city-wide celebration of craft beer featuring events, tastings, and special releases at breweries and bars across Denver.

Wine And Cocktail Bars

- **Williams & Graham:** A speakeasy-style bar offering creative cocktails.
- **Infinite Monkey Theorem:** An urban winery with a relaxed atmosphere.
- **Asbury Provisions:** A cocktail emporium and craft beer bar in one with
- **BEZEL Denver:** Located in the Sheraton Denver Downtown Hotel, The BEZEL is opulent and offers inventive drinks and small plates
- **Welton Room:** With an L.A. vibe this Five Points cocktail lounge is one of the best looking night spots in the neighborhood
- **The Cruise Room:** A historic bar inside the Oxford Hotel, styled after a bar on the Queen Mary.

The Cruise Room

CHAPTER 8: SHOPPING IN DENVER

16th Street Mall
A pedestrian-friendly street lined with shops, restaurants, and entertainment options. Hop on the free shuttle to explore the length of the mall.

Cherry Creek Shopping Center

An upscale shopping destination with over 160 stores, including luxury brands and department stores. Adjacent to the shopping center is Cherry Creek North, a charming area with boutiques, galleries, and dining.

Denver Pavilions

Located on the 16th Street Mall, Denver Pavilions offers a mix of shopping, dining, and entertainment options, including a movie theater and a bowling alley. It's a great spot for a fun day out in the city.

Denver Pavilions

Belmar

An "al fresco" shopping and dining area, Belmar is just a few minutes from downtown, and offers more than 75 stores and restaurants and also a bowling alley.

Denver Premium Outlets

This fairly new outlet mall offers a mix of popular and lifestyle brands at a discounted price. It also has a one-of-a-kind outdoor play area, featuring a climbing tower, slides, grassy foothills, stepping stones and even a dinosaur fossil pit, so the kids will love it too.

The Shops at Northfield

The Shops at Northfield is an open-air shopping, dining and entertainment destination which includes many anchor stores, a movie theater, comedy club and more than 60 specialty shops and restaurants.

Indoor malls include: The Colorado Mills Mall, Park Meadows Mall, and the Aurora Mall

Bonus: Local Boutiques and Unique Shops

There are plenty to choose from that will provide visitors with a one-of-a kind experience. A few of these include Tattered Cover Book Store, Rockmount Ranch Wear, Inspyre Boutique Common Threads, or check out The Dairy Block area for unique food and finds.

The Dairy Block

CHAPTER 9: ARTS AND ENTERTAINMENT

Performing Arts Venues

Denver Performing Arts Complex
One of the largest performing arts centers in the country, it hosts Broadway shows, operas, ballets, and symphonies.

Paramount Theatre
A historic venue featuring concerts, comedy shows, and film screenings.

Ellie Caulkins Opera House
Known for its stunning architecture and world-class performances.

"Dancers" Sculpture at the Denver Performing Arts Complex

Live Music Hotspots

Living in Denver and being a part of the amazing music scene has been a true privilege. My husband and I have been lucky enough to attend hundreds of music shows and events from huge concert experiences to smaller, more intimate spots. Take some time to catch a show at one of the local unique venues. Here are a few favorites.

The Bluebird Theater

An intimate venue with a rich history, hosting a variety of live music acts.

The Fillmore Auditorium

A popular venue for larger concerts, featuring a wide range of genres.

Ogden Theatre

Another historic venue offering an eclectic lineup of performances.

The Grizzly Rose

With its rustic Western decor, The Grizzly Rose offers an authentic country experience and features live country music performances.

Cervantes Masterpiece Ballroom

Another favorite local spot, this venue features a wide range of musical genres including funk, electronic, hip-hop, and electronic.

The Bluebird Theater

Popular Night Clubs

Temple Nightclub

Located in downtown Denver, Temple Nightclub offers a unique experience with its multi-level layout and stunning decor. It features a variety of music genres, from EDM to hip-hop, and often features internationally recognized DJs.

The Church Nightclub

Located in a converted church building, The Church Nightclub offers a truly unique ambiance. It has multiple dance floors and hosts a diverse range of events, including electronic music, hip-hop, and themed parties.

Vinyl Nightclub

Vinyl is a popular nightclub in Denver that focuses on underground electronic music. It has a more intimate setting compared to some larger clubs and often showcases local and up-and-coming DJs.

Tracks Nightclub

Tracks is a well-established LGBTQ+ nightclub in Denver, known for its inclusive and welcoming environment. It features multiple dance floors and hosts a variety of events, including drag shows and themed parties.

Bar Standard and Milk Bar

Located in the historic South of Colfax district, Bar Standard/Milk Bar is known for its eclectic music selection, ranging from electronic to live bands. It offers a laid-back atmosphere and is a favorite among locals.

Bar Standard & Milk Bar

Annual Festivals And Events

Denver Film Festival

Celebrating independent and international films, this festival attracts cinephiles from around the world.

Great American Beer Festival

The largest beer festival in the U.S., showcasing thousands of beers from hundreds of breweries.

The Great American Beer Festival

Denver PrideFest

One of the largest LGBTQ+ pride events in the country, featuring parades, concerts, and cultural activities.

A Taste of Colorado

A beloved annual festival that celebrates the food, art, music, and cultural heritage of Colorado.

CHAPTER 10: DAY TRIPS AND EXCURSIONS

While there is plenty to do in Denver alone, Colorado is way too beautiful to miss out on all of the surrounding stunning, natural beauty and historical sites.

Boulder, Colorado

Just a 30-minute drive from Denver, the free-spirited college town of Boulder offers outdoor activities, a charming downtown, and the beautiful Flatirons. An area I often visit with guests is Pearl Street Mall and Chautauqua Park.

Golden, Colorado

Golden is a historic town with a picturesque downtown and access to outdoor adventures like hiking and tubing on

Clear Creek. Don't forget to take a tour of the Coors Brewery, the largest single site brewery in the world.

Colorado Springs and Pikes Peak

An hour south of Denver, Colorado Springs boasts attractions like the beautiful Garden of the Gods, the U.S. Air Force Academy, and the scenic drive up to Pikes Peak.

Garden of the Gods, Colorado Springs

Estes Park

Gateway to Rocky Mountain National Park, Estes Park offers stunning scenery, hiking trails, and wildlife viewing. The town itself has quaint shops and restaurants along their Main Street area.

Breckenridge and Other Mountain Towns

Explore the charming mountain town of Breckenridge, known for its ski resort, historic district, and vibrant arts scene. Other nearby mountain towns worth visiting include Vail, Aspen, and Winter Park.

Ski Slope at Breckenridge Ski Resort

CHAPTER 11: SAFETY TIPS AND LOCAL ETIQUETTE

Health And Safety Tips

- Altitude Sickness: Denver is a mile high, so drink plenty of water and take it easy when you first arrive to acclimate.
- Weather: Denver experiences rapid weather changes. Always check the forecast and dress in layers.
- The sun is intense: Along with the 300 days of sunshine a year and the altitude, getting a sunburn can easily happen. Please wear SPF and dress in light layers.
- Hydrate, hydrate, hydrate: Drink more water than you think. The low humidity makes the air extremely dry. Staying hydrated will help with altitude sickness, endurance, (and even keep you from getting drunk quicker if you're enjoying an alcoholic beverage)

Local Customs And Etiquette

- Tipping: You can expect extra restaurant fees for a number of restaurants. Since Covid, Denver restaurants have increasingly added a pre-tax "cost-of-living fee" to the dining bill to supplement staff wages. In general, if the fee is 12% or less, a gratuity is still expected and very much appreciated.
- Denverites are generally super friendly and open to having a chat with strangers. We're a diverse group, so just keep the politics out of it and don't assume people share your opinion.
- Marijuana: Recreational use is legal for adults 21 and over, but consumption is restricted to private residences. Public consumption is prohibited. Please only purchase from a dispensary.
- No Pressure to Dress Up: Casual dress is completely fine in Denver. You'll find most Denverites in T-shirts, jeans or yoga pants, a puffy jacket, and comfy sneakers or sandals.

Useful Apps And Websites

https://www.denver.org/
The official tourism site with event listings, travel tips, and more.

https://www.rtd-denver.com/fares-passes/mobile-ticketing
RTD Mobile Ticketing: For buying and using tickets for Denver's public transportation.

https://www.yelp.com/
Yelp: For finding restaurant reviews and recommendations.

Emergency Contacts

- Police: 911 (emergency), 720-913-2000 (non-emergency)
- Medical: 911 (emergency), 303-436-6000 (Denver Health Hospital)
- Tourist Information: Visit Denver Information Center, 303-892-1505

CONCLUSION

I hope you've found inspiration and excitement for your upcoming adventures in Denver. With its rich history, deep culture, and breathtaking natural beauty, Denver offers an endless array of experiences waiting to be discovered. Whether you're savoring the flavors of its culinary scene, exploring the stunning Rocky Mountains, or immersing yourself in the local arts and music, Denver promises to leave a lasting impression, just like it has for my family throughout the last decade and a half.

Each neighborhood has its unique charm, and each excursion offers a new perspective on what makes this city so special. The warm and welcoming spirit of Denverites will make you feel at home, whether you're visiting for a weekend or a while.

As you plan your trip, remember to embrace the unexpected and take the time to venture off the beaten path. The hidden gems and local favorites often hold the most memorable moments. Denver is a city that thrives on exploration and discovery, and I hope you enjoy every step of your journey.

Thank you for choosing this guide to accompany you on your travels. May your experiences in Denver be filled with unforgettable memories. Safe travels, and welcome to the Mile High City!

◆ ◆ ◆

If you found this book helpful, I would really appreciate it if you could leave a favorable review on Amazon. Thank you for your support!

Howdy from Colorado!

RESOURCES

Delicious Denver Food Tours. (2024, March 21). *37 things to do in Denver in winter - Delicious Denver food Tours*. https://www.deliciousdenverfoodtours.com/blogs/thingstodoindenverinwinter/

Trip, B. Y. (n.d.). *How much do hotels cost in Denver? Hotel prices for Denver, Colorado | Budget your trip*. Budget Your Trip. https://www.budgetyourtrip.com/hotels/united-states-of-america/denver-5419384

Visit Denver Convention and Visitors Bureau. (2024). *Denver Neighborhood Guide | VISIT DENVER*. Denver.org. Retrieved June 27, 2024, from https://www.denver.org/neighborhoods/

Collins, J. (2021, May 19). *First-Time traveling to Denver: 11 things you need to know. dfwt*. https://www.denverfreewalkingtours.com/post/11-things-you-need-to-know

Denver Shopping | VISIT DENVER. (n.d.). https://www.denver.org/things-to-do/shopping/

Martin, M. (2024, May 23). *The ten best places to eat breakfast in Denver. Westword*. https://www.westword.com/restaurants/best-breakfast-in-denver-colorado-20369970

Prado, L. (2023, July 19). 16 things to know before visiting

Denver. *Lonely Planet.* https://www.lonelyplanet.com/ articles/things-to-know-before-traveling-to-denver

Printed in Great Britain
by Amazon